A

from the Brooklyn Children's Museum

AMERICAN DOLLS

from the Brooklyn Children's Museum

Edited by Susan Feuer

Ariel Books
Andrews and McMeel
Kansas City

ISBN: 0-8362-3127-9
Library of Congress Catalog Card Number: (TK)

INTRODUCTION

There are few things as universally well loved as dolls. Made from every material imaginable—wax, leaves, wood, terra-cotta, lead, even shoes—dolls have been created by nearly every culture in the world. However, they were not thought of as children's toys until a few hundred years ago; ancient dolls were created as talismans, fetishes, and idols.

Today, dolls are a big business in America and other parts of the world. Adults spend millions of dollars a year on them as presents for children and as collectibles for themselves. There are doll clubs, doll magazines, doll fairs, and even doll conventions. Of course, it hasn't always been this way in America. When the first colonists came to America they brought handmade dolls with them. Those who wanted fine (and expensive) dolls imported them from Europe, but the majority of new Americans couldn't afford to do that, so they continued to make their dolls at home. These folk dolls were the only kinds of dolls made in America for hundreds of years; American dolls weren't produced commercially until the late nineteenth century.

and apples grew in nearly every part of the country so there were always plenty available to use for dolls. Since dried apples are naturally wrinkled, these dolls were often made to resemble elderly people. Dried apples and nuts are still used today in rural parts of America to make dolls that are full of character and humor.

Rag dolls were one of the most common types of folk dolls made by the early American settlers and the generations to follow. Even the poorest of families had rags, which could be stitched together to form dolls whose charm and simplicity endeared them to their owners. One particularly interesting rag doll is made by the Amish, who believe it is a sin to capture their likenesses in photographs, paintings, or dolls. Hence, Amish rag dolls have no facial features, and they are always dressed in the typical, dark-colored clothing favored by this sect.

The industrial revolution, which reached America by the mid–nineteenth century, changed doll making from a folk craft into an industry. The new factories that sprang up enabled dolls to be mass produced in America for the first time, and many American industrial innovations of this period translated into innovations in doll manufacturing as well. For instance, in 1844, Charles Goodyear patented the process of vulcanization, which made rubber elastic, strong, and stable. Seven years later, Goodyear's brother patented a rubber doll's head and the rubber baby doll was born.

The growth of textile mills around this time led to the invention of printed cloth dolls. Patterns were sold inexpensively by the yard and the dolls were cut out, sewn, and stuffed at home. One of the first companies to sell printed fabric patterns was the Arnold Print Works of North Adams, Massachusetts, which produced patterns for dolls and animals. In the twentieth century, it was common for companies such as Kellogg's to offer printed fabric dolls as promotional premiums.

Another doll-making innovation in the mid–nineteenth century was the use of papier-mâché, which had been used earlier for making European dolls, but its popularity had waned. However, Ludwig Greiner, a German immigrant living in Philadelphia, brought papier-mâché dolls back into fashion with his American creations. The papier-mâché dolls, for which Greiner obtained a patent in 1858, were made from a mixture of paper, whiting (a powder made from crushed calcium carbonate) flour, and glue. Greiner's papier-mâché was durable and lightweight, and his dolls were an improvement over the European papier-mâché ones.

One of America's most famous and innovative doll makers was Albert Schoenhut, also a German immigrant. Though the material he used, wood, was not an innovation in doll making, what he did with it was: his wooden dolls had steel spring hinges in their joints that allowed them to be placed in natural poses, thus resembling real children engaged in everyday activities. Schoenhut, who also invented a toy piano and a Humpty Dumpty circus, patented his design for wooden dolls in 1911.

lowed. Celluloid, a synthetic plastic-like material, had been used for making dolls before plastic, but it had many drawbacks, the worst being its flammability. Madame Alexander, one of the first doll makers to use hard plastic, produced dolls modeled after Shirley Temple, Snow White, Scarlett O'Hara, and many others. The Barbie doll, patented in 1958 by Mattel, was first made of plastic and then of vinyl, another synthetic material. Barbie dolls, with their high fashion wardrobes, were instantly popular and remain so today.

This book traces the history of American dolls and touches upon important landmarks in American doll making.

All the photographs and information about dolls were provided by the Brooklyn Children's Museum, founded in 1899 as the first children's museum in the world. The museum's approximately twenty-five-hundred doll collection includes samples of handmade ethnic dolls from nearly every part of the world.

Dolls provide comfort, amusement, fantasy, and pleasure to us both as children and adults. Whether you are a doll collector, or just a doll lover, you will be sure to enjoy reading about the American dolls collected in this lovely little volume.

Lady Doll

Ludwig Greiner
Philadelphia, Pennsylvania
c. 1860

This 30 1/2-inch tall Ludwig Greiner doll has a papier-mâché head and cloth body. Greiner immigrated from Germany to Philadelphia in the mid–nineteenth century and applied his doll making skills to the manufacture of American dolls. This doll is not wearing its original clothing; it was redressed in the 1960s after the clothing deteriorated.

AMERICAN DOLLS

PRE-GREINER DOLL

Region unknown
c. 1850

This is a pre-Greiner papier-mâché doll with a cloth body. Though not much is known about this doll, its corkscrew curls and middle part suggest a mid–nineteenth century manufacture date.

AMERICAN DOLLS

RUBBER DOLL

Goodyear Rubber Company
Connecticut
1850s

Black rubber dolls made by the Goodyear Rubber Company are extremely rare, as most of them deteriorated and were discarded. The first Goodyear dolls were patented in 1844 when the process of vulcanization made it possible to produce a hard rubber doll. Some of these rubber dolls were painted white.

AMERICAN DOLLS

RUBBER BOY

Sun Rubber Company
Ohio
c. 1938

Ruth E. Newton designed this rubber doll for the Sun Rubber Company of Barberton, Ohio. Rubber dolls were desirable toys for children because they were durable, washable, and inexpensive. This boy doll has a squeaker in his left leg.

AMERICAN DOLLS

WOODEN BOY

Albert Schoenhut
Philadelphia, Pennsylvania
c. 1915

Albert Schoenhut was a German toy maker who came to Philadelphia in 1866 to work for the Wanamaker Department Store. This eighteen-inch doll is one of his famous wooden dolls constructed with steel spring joints, which enabled the dolls to stand in various natural poses without falling over. The tattered clothes are original.

❧

AMERICAN DOLLS

MARTHA WASHINGTON DOLL

※

Mrs. Margaret Finch
New Rochelle, New York
1955

Made on commission for the Brooklyn Children's Museum, this is a hand-carved wooden portrait doll. (A portrait doll is a doll modeled after a real person.) The label reads "Peggy Lenape," the name doll-maker Margaret Finch used for her early dolls. Her dolls are known for their realism and accuracy, down to the smallest detail.

✳

AMERICAN DOLLS

PRINTED CLOTH DOLL

Region unknown
1900–1910

With the development of lithography in the late nineteenth century the mass production of printed cloth dolls became possible. Sold as an inexpensive printed pattern, the doll was then cut out, stuffed, and sewn at home. Many printed dolls were produced as advertising premiums and souvenirs.

AMERICAN DOLLS

PRINTED CLOTH MAN

Region unknown
c. 1900

This is a composite doll made from parts of at least three other dolls. The printed cloth face, rag body, and china hands are an unusual, though attractive, combination.

AMERICAN DOLLS

COMPOSITION DOLL

❧❧❧

Region unknown
Early Twentieth Century

Composition, pressed wood pulp that has been glazed and painted, became a popular alternative to bisque in the early twentieth century because it was durable and relatively inexpensive. Not much is known about this doll or composition dolls in general since they were rarely marked with the manufacturer's name. This one has blue glass eyes, kidskin arms, and a cloth body.

❦
AMERICAN DOLLS

COMPOSITION DOLL

Ideal Toy Corporation
Brooklyn, New York
c. 1920

The Ideal Toy Corporation was a leading manufacturer of composition dolls. This one has a red wig and blue eyes that shut when it is laid down. The head is composition, the legs and body are cloth, and a voice box in the body says Mama when the doll is turned over. The costume is original.

AMERICAN DOLLS

PATSYETTE

&

EFFanBEE
New York, New York
c. 1931

EFFanBEE's Patsyette first appeared in 1931 and was an addition to the general line of Patsy dolls that EFFanBEE (the trade name for Fleischaker & Baum) had been producing since 1924. This all-composition doll has a red mohair wig.

AMERICAN DOLLS

SHIRLEY TEMPLE

Ideal Toy Corporation
Brooklyn, New York
c. 1935

This is an all-composition Shirley Temple doll made by the Ideal Toy Corporation. From 1934 to 1940 this type of Shirley Temple doll was made in a variety of sizes with costumes based on her movies. Since Shirley Temple was the most popular movie star in the world at that time, the dolls were a great success.

AMERICAN DOLLS

SKIPPY COWBOY

EFFanBEE
New York, New York
c. 1935

EFFanBEE created the first composition Skippy doll in 1929. Based on a comic strip character originated by Percy Crosby, Skippy was advertised as the boyfriend of the popular EFFanBEE girl doll, Patsy.

AMERICAN DOLLS

SEATED KEWPIE

Rose O'Neill
United States and Germany
c. 1913

This is an original bisque Kewpie doll designed by Rose O'Neill. The word "kewpie" is a play on words meaning "little cupid"; the doll was based on O'Neill's illustrated children's verses that appeared in *Ladies' Home Journal*. Insufficient patent protection enabled other companies to use the name and to manufacture similar dolls.

AMERICAN DOLLS

GIRL DOLL

Fulper Pottery Company
Flemington, New Jersey
1918–1922

Made by the Fulper Pottery Company, this girl doll has a bisque head. Until they were forced to shut down during World War I, the majority of bisque dolls were produced in French and German factories. The Fulper Pottery Company helped fill the demand for bisque dolls for six years but stopped production when the European factories were re-opened.

American Dolls

Bye-Lo Baby

Grace Storey Putnam
United States and Germany
c. 1925

This baby doll was designed by Grace Storey Putnam and was modeled after a three-day-old infant, which accounts for its realistic appearance. Bye-Lo baby dolls were an instant success and were one of the most popular dolls ever made. Although some Bye-Lo dolls were made with composition heads, this one has a bisque head.

AMERICAN DOLLS

LADY DOLL

Emma C. Clear
California
c. 1940

This doll was made by Emma C. Clear; it is a reproduction of late nineteenth century French and German fashion dolls. Only the hands and head are bisque; the rest is cloth. Clear began her career repairing and dressing dolls and then moved on to designing and manufacturing them. Clear dolls are usually marked with her name and the date of production on the shoulder.

AMERICAN DOLLS

Sonja Henie Doll

Madame Alexander
New York, New York
c. 1940

Madame Alexander, perhaps the best-known American doll maker, began making Sonja Henie dolls in 1939. This one is made of hard plastic and wears its original costume. Sonja Henie was an extremely popular Olympic skating champion who became even more popular after she became a movie star.

✳

AMERICAN DOLLS

MARMEE DOLL

Madame Alexander
New York, New York
1954

Based on the classic Louisa May Alcott book, this Madame Alexander *Little Women* doll is made of hard plastic with a swivel head. Alexander produced sets of *Little Women* dolls between 1948 and 1956 with variations in size and costume.

AMERICAN DOLLS

BETSY ROSS

✳

Kimcraft
Independence, Missouri
1940s

Kimcraft, a company established in 1940, commissioned folk and ethnic dolls from folk artists throughout the United States. This Betsy Ross doll has a clay head and arms; it is one of a series of historical portrait dolls that the company produced.

✳

American Dolls

SEMINOLE WOMAN

Seminole Indians, Florida
c. 1910–1920

Made from palmetto fiber, a variety of palm tree that grows in the southern United States, this brightly attired Seminole doll is dressed in patchwork clothing, and though it appears to be wearing a bonnet, it is not; the doll's hairstyle is copied from Seminole women, who comb their hair over wood frames so it looks as if they're wearing wide-brimmed hats.

AMERICAN DOLLS

BUTTERFLY MAIDEN DOLL

Hopi Indians, Arizona
c. 1910–1920

Dressed in a Butterfly Maiden costume, this wooden doll is from a Hopi reservation in Arizona. The doll's attire represents the costumes that unmarried Hopi girls wear while dancing in ceremonies seeking rain for crops and fertility.

AMERICAN DOLLS

CRADLEBOARD DOLL

❧

Paiute Indians, Nevada
c. 1920

This Paiute cradleboard and doll is
from the Yerlington Colony and
Reservation in Nevada. The cradleboard is made from wicker and cloth
and is modeled after a real cradleboard, traditionally used to carry
infants. The rubber doll was not
made by a Paiute; it was obtained in
a trade.

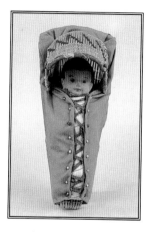

AMERICAN DOLLS

CHEROKEE WOMAN

❀

Cherokee Indians, North Carolina
1965

This wooden doll was made by Joe Owl, a well-known Cherokee doll maker, whose signature appears on the sole of the doll's right foot. Owl made many dolls; all of them are meticulously carved and elaborately dressed, and represent people engaged in everyday activities.

❀

AMERICAN DOLLS

WOODEN FOLK DOLL

New England
c. 1850

As it is made from three different materials, this antique doll may have been assembled from parts of other dolls. It has a hand-carved and painted wooden head, a handmade cloth body, and bisque hands.

AMERICAN DOLLS

WOMAN WITH CHURN NUT DOLL

Tennessee Mountains
1950s

Because nuts are plentiful, sturdy, and easily painted, many folk dolls were made with nut heads. This one has a hickory-nut head, wooden hands, and a cloth body. It is seated and holding a butter churn.

AMERICAN DOLLS

WOMAN WITH CHILD NUT DOLL

❦

Kentucky Mountains
Late Nineteenth Century

Freed slaves turned their doll-making talents into a source of income after the Civil War. This elderly, black nut-head woman and cloth child are dressed in their finest clothes: the woman is wearing a silk dress and cape. This is an early example of a folk doll that has survived intact.

♥
AMERICAN DOLLS

CORK AND NET DOLL

California
c. 1950

Cork and fishnet are the only materials used in the construction of this doll. It is a good example of the way in which doll makers use any materials available to them when exercising their craft.

AMERICAN DOLLS

SHELL GIRL

Captain and Mrs. L. J. Layton
Florida
c. 1935

Captain and Mrs. L. J. Layton, a retired Florida couple, collected shells along the Gulf Coast for their dolls. He constructed their bodies; she painted them and made their accessories. This shell doll is a flower girl and is part of a wedding party.

AMERICAN DOLLS

DRIED APPLE TEACHER DOLL

Region unknown
1930–1940

Dried apple-head dolls are a legacy of Native American doll makers. Since dried apples have naturally wrinkled surfaces, they are often used to make elderly looking dolls. This doll has a dried-apple head and hands, a cloth body, and lamb's wool hair.

AMERICAN DOLLS

Nut and Leaf Folk Doll

Southern United States
c. 1930

This is an elaborate nut-head and tobacco-leaf doll. Any types of leaves that do not dry out and become brittle can be used for making dolls. Banana and palm leaves are common doll materials in other parts of the world.

AMERICAN DOLLS

Black Rag Doll

❧

Jackson, Mississippi
1968

This is a contemporary rag doll made by the Jackson Mississippi Co-op, an outgrowth of the 1960s Civil Rights Movement, which gave impetus to the revival and continuation of southern crafts.